the Companion DISCUSSION GUIDE for the ATF Teen Devo magazine

[Issue 2 • Volume 1]

NE✗GEN®

Building the New Generation of Believers

COOK COMMUNICATIONS MINISTRIES
Colorado Springs, Colorado • Paris, Ontario
KINGSWAY COMMUNICATIONS LTD
Eastbourne, England

NexGen® is an imprint of
Cook Communications Ministries, Colorado Springs, CO 80918
Cook Communications, Paris, Ontario
Kingsway Communications, Eastbourne, England

THE COMPANION DISCUSSION GUIDE FOR THE ATF TEEN DEVO MAGAZINE
©2005 by Cook Communications Ministries

First printing, 2005
Printed in the United States of America
1 2 3 4 5 6 7 8 9 10 Printing Year 09 08 07 06 05

Content: Frieda Nossaman
Editor: Mary Grace Becker
Cover Design: Brand Navigation
Interior Design: Helen Harrison

INTRODUCTION

Teens have a hard life. You, as their youth leader, know this. Making the grades, succeeding in sports, work, and relationships requires effort and a certain maturity and finesse. High expectations from parents, teachers, coaches—and unrealistic expectations from the media—make for a tricky road to maneuver. For many, just getting through high school with one's self-esteem intact is the ultimate survivor story.

Although all teens need friends, your role as youth leader needs to be much more. The key to working with teens comes down to this: care for them, be a good listener and someone they can trust and learn from. Above all, pray for them by name each week. Allow your teens to share their feelings without interrupting and analyzing their every word. An open heart towards them is the best gift you can give.

This *Companion Discussion Guide* is for use with the *Acquire the Fire Teen Devo* magazine, Issue 2. Take time to familiarize yourself with the magazine before meeting with your group. The magazine's informal approach invites teens to look inside and discover God's wisdom, wonder, and love for them. The sessions in this discussion guide will allow you to help your teens get a handle on their thoughts and feelings and learn from the process of examining them.

Each session is divided into three sections: **Beginning**, **Middle** and **End**. It doesn't get simpler than that! The **Beginning** may include an optional activity to grab the interest of the group. If you choose not to do it, go ahead with the lesson. It's your choice. Open with prayer asking God to unite your group, making your time together one of trust and concern for one another. After the prayer, move ahead to the discussion questions.

The **Middle** takes you into the heart of *Acquire the Fire*. Some sessions focus on segments in the Guys' section and others in the Girls' section of the devo. Have everyone in the group turn to the page and look at it together. Use the suggested questions to get the ball rolling. The **End** gives everyone a chance to reflect on how the issues you've raised affect each person individually. Close your time together with the prayer provided (or use your own). Be sure to answer any questions your teens might have.

Music is very important to teens. Play it in the background or to open prayer times. Food makes a great icebreaker too. Oh, don't forget to encourage teens to bring their Bibles. Leading a group of teens takes energy, attention, commitment, and a sense of humor. God applauds your effort with his teenagers, as do we!

Before you start,

here are brief descriptions of the devotions found inside the *Acquire the Fire Devo* magazine. They expand on the five topics for Issue 2: purpose, values, self-worth, materialism, and motivation in Christ. The devo titles below repeat by section, but vary by topic.

■ Devo 1: Need2Know

This devo focuses on what the Bible says on the topic.

■ Devo 2: GODfidential

This devo expresses the view of a youth pastor or a youth worker.

■ Devo 3: girl-OUTstanding or MAN-datory

This devo reflects on what makes a godly man or woman on fire for Christ.

■ Devo 4: UP/IN/OUT

This devo contains a Scripture passage that teaches a discipleship principle. UP—how it relates to our relationship with God; IN—how it relates to our relationship with other believers; and OUT—how it relates to our relationship with nonbelievers.

■ Devo 5: Truth and Dare

This devo is divided in two: A "Truth"—a Scripture passage related to the topic and a paragraph that ties the Scripture to today's teens. And a "Dare" section—strongly worded challenge to the teen to take the truth of the Scripture and make a stand for Christ.

■ Devo 6: Faith on Fire

How faith is key to dealing with each topic.

■ Devo 7: The Super Natural Power of Prayer

Well-worded prayers for teens to use.

■ Generation My

Christian girls answer teen questions.

■ Tribal Wisdom

Christian guys answer teen questions.

And there you have it!
Lesson 1 is straight ahead.

DIVINE PURPOSE

Bible Truth:
In God our purpose is defined.

Bible Verse:
"Now it is God who makes us stand firm in Christ. He anointed us" (2 Corinthians 1:21).

Stuff:
Bibles, paper, pens, crackers, cheese, cream cheese spread, pepperoni circles, sliced olives and mushrooms, pimentos, knives, napkins

BEGINNING

As you start your group time, remember that no matter whether you're an experienced leader or a novice, it's not up to you to transform a life for Christ. Only God can do that. Your commitment and relationship will be the things that bring your teens back week after week. Begin your devotional time by asking God to direct your meeting and help your teens as they journey to discover his purpose for them. Invite members of your group to share prayer requests if they have them. Pray aloud for these requests.

Set out the ingredients (listed in the "Stuff" section on p. 5) that you have brought today. Have teens pair up. Hand one teen from each pair a piece of paper and a pen and instruct him or her to write the steps for making a unique snack creation using the food items provided. Don't allow the partner to help or look at what the other person is writing. Say, **The purpose of this little exercise is to see how well your directions help your partner make a delicious snack. When you are finished writing have your partner follow your directions *exactly* as they are written.** It will be humorous to see how many snack creations actually turn out like they are supposed to. Discuss:

Q. How difficult was it to write instructions for something that required many steps? Did you think what you were writing was clear and to the point? Did your partner? Explain.

A. Teens may mention that it seemed a simple assignment, but the reality of it was much more difficult. Teens also may note that by following the instructions *exactly*, their partner did things in making the sandwich that they as writers didn't anticipate.

Optional Activity

Place a large beach ball in the center of your room or space. Instruct teens to form a line (from front to back). Assign the first person in line the task of leading the line behind him or her creatively, for example, skipping, hopping, dancing, etc. The only requirement is that they somehow incorporate the ball into the group setting. Allow a few different teens to lead and have fun observing what kinds of things they do as leaders. Conclude the activity by mentioning that all of the leaders led with purpose and got the people behind them to follow. Mention that like this activity, in life, God leads us—sometimes in ways we don't always want to go.

Q. How difficult was it to *follow* the directions exactly? Did any of you find that your partner forgot an essential instruction—such as "use a *knife* to spread the cream cheese"? Explain your experience.

A. Teens may mention that following the directions *exactly* was difficult because they already have a preconceived idea of what a good snack is *supposed* to look like. Some may say the directions weren't clear or were incomplete, etc.

Summarize by saying: If giving directions for making snacks is this difficult, aren't you glad you aren't the one directing the purpose of your own life? God steers us through his perfect Word so we can find out why we're here. If we follow his directives, we can be sure we are going the way he intended.

MIDDLE

Have teens turn to "Faith on Fire" Choose or Lose on page 9 of the Girls' section of *Acquire the Fire,* Issue 2. Call on a few teens to read it aloud. Discuss:

Q. Why do you think the blame of sin falls on Adam and Eve for messing up a perfect universe? Do you think you would have done things differently if you had been them?

A. It's easy to play the blame-game when it comes to the first man and woman. After all, it was just a piece of fruit. But we have to remember that it was the idea of rebelling against God and wishing to be as wise as he is that really got them to fall hard. Those are the same kinds of sins we often fall into today; things really haven't changed that much after all.

Q. Why do you think it is God's purpose to give us the freedom to choose?

A. God doesn't want to force his creations to submit to him; he wants us to desire to. Being a part of God's plan actually comes down to three words: faith, trust, and obedience.

Q. In Genesis 3:14-15 we get a hint that Jesus' purpose will be to overthrow Satan. How do you think the promise of Jesus made Adam and Eve feel?

A. God tells of one who will one day overthrow Satan and make a way for sinners to come back to God. That person is Jesus Christ. It must have been a relief to Adam and Eve to know that the consequences of their sin against all humanity would not last forever. One day Jesus would change everything. Adam and Eve may have felt discouraged, but they (and those who would come after them) could still find purpose—in Jesus.

END

Have everyone turn to "Truth & Dare" Suicide—A Losing Cause for Teens on page 12 in the Girls' section of *Acquire the Fire.* Have one teen read the "Truth" section and have another teen read the "Dare" section.

Mention that suicide is *never* God's purpose. He doesn't want "anyone to perish" (die), 2 Peter 3:9. This verse is talking about spiritual death, but it could encompass physical death as well. **Just as God commands us not to murder (Exodus 20:13), we also have no right to end our lives. Suicide is wrong because it takes away—from God and others—a life that was meant to be lived.**

Suicide is wrong because it takes away from God and others a life that was meant to be lived.

Be sensitive to the fact that some teens may know of people who have taken their own lives; a rare few may even have family members that have done so. Explain to teens that although they can help people who contemplate suicide, they are not responsible for another's actions. Contemplate as a group:

Q. Why do you think Satan celebrates when a teenager chooses to end his or her life?

A. Suicide is the rare occasion when Satan seemingly wins.

Q. Why might a teenager feel that death is his or her only out?

A. Some teens might seem surprised by the stats about suicide but others may not, noting that the world seems a terrible place to many people, especially non-Christians, and they may see death as an escape from pain. Reiterate the fact that suicide is never an acceptable out. There is always someone who can help—no matter how dire a person's circumstances may seem. Statistics have shown that talking about suicide will *not* make teens think about committing it; rather, it will do the opposite. Many teens contemplate suicide but have no real intention of ever committing it. On the other hand, teens commit suicide because they feel that no one cares about them—or the extent of their pain. By discussing this sensitive subject with your teens, you can reassure them about how much you, as their leader, care for them. Be sure to mention others who care as well, such as their friends, family, and, most of all, their Heavenly Father.

Q. Are there things teens can do to help troubled teens find a reason to celebrate life?

A. Answers will vary, but may include: encouraging them, taking an interest in them, complimenting them, being aware of changes that occur in their lives, praying for them, helping them see the strengths that you see, etc.

Say, **God has a purpose for you. How do you discover it? Read God's Word in search of real answers for real-life questions. His promise is that you'll discover who you are in the process.**

Life is difficult and those we love sometimes become unsettled as a result. Be aware of the signs of depression in a friend, brother or sister. And don't be afraid to mention it to others. You may not be alone in your observations and, together, something can be done to help.

Have a teen look up today's verse found in 2 Corinthians 1:21.

"Now it is God who makes us stand firm in Christ. He anointed us." Mention that our purpose in life comes from standing firm in Christ and what he has already accomplished on the cross on our behalf. God not only has a purpose for each of us, but he has claimed us as his own. He also doesn't just leave us hanging but sent his Holy Spirit to guide and direct us. Most of all, God guarantees that if we believe in him, then we have a future worth living for. It is with divine purpose—a purpose much higher than our own ways of doing things—that we need to live our lives.

Close in prayer. Encourage teens to add their thoughts as well.

Lord, we long to be people of purpose. Help us discover it for our lives. Create in us a clean heart and the burning desire to know and love you above all things. Your very real existence gives us hope and a future. Thank you for the gift of our birth and your promise to travel with us all the days of our lives. In Jesus' name, amen.

IN GOD'S WILL— THERE'S A WAY

Purpose

Bible Truth:
Our future rests in God's hands.

Bible Verse:
"I cry out to God Most High, to God, who fulfills his purpose for me" (Psalm 57:2).

Stuff: Bibles, a comfortable place (couch, beanbag chair, pillows, comforters, blankets, large stuffed animals, etc.)

LESSON TWO

BEGINNING

As you begin your devotional time together, pray and ask God to help you lead and encourage your group as they seek God's will for their lives. Invite members of your group to share prayer requests. Ask one or two in the group to pray aloud for the requests that have been shared.

Have group members come settle in a comfortable area. Go around and ask each person to share his or her childhood dreams. In other words, what each wanted to be when they "grew up." Don't allow anyone to make fun of another person and be sensitive that some teens might feel uncomfortable sharing. After all teens have had a chance to talk, go back around the group and ask if their goals were still the same. Give ample time for teens to explain themselves. Finally, go back around the group and ask teens who no longer have those same life goals what they now would like to do with their future. (This activity will give you insight into your teens' hopes and dreams. Be sure to jot down who wants to do what somewhere in a journal or notebook and refer to it from time to time as the issue of goals or future plans comes up.)

Optional Activity

Invite teens to call out anything they want in life that might tie in to what God's will could be for them, for example, "being a doctor," "running a children's camp," "getting married and having kids," "being a writer," "studying the law," "becoming an electrical engineer," etc. Write the responses down on a poster board or white board. There are no right answers, but this activity will get your group thinking about what it means to be working in the world within God's will. It isn't just the, "be a missionary overseas," "go to seminary," answers that some teens might expect. Their peers may have keen insight into what God's will looks like for them.

Say, **To the eyes of unbelievers, Jesus' life on earth appears a total failure. Although a master teacher in his day, Jesus' early death demonstrated to many a misguided life. Yet, in Scripture, Jesus is called "the Christ," a title that means "anointed one." His remarkable story survives because of the purposeful intent of believers to communicate both orally and in written word his life-saving message.**

"I cry out to God Most High, to God who fulfills his purpose for me."
(Psalm 57:2)

MIDDLE

Read the question and answer from "Tribal Wisdom" page 6 in the Guys' section of *Acquire the Fire,* Issue 2:

Q. I hear all the time…seek out God's will for your life. Here's my question: just where am I supposed to find God's will?

Kelly (15)

A. Dear Kelly,
God is the ultimate decision-maker. With his will in mind, he sets out to make the right decision that will fit your life perfectly. So for starters start by reading the Bible. Sure, you've heard it a million times, but have you actually done it? God's Word and will for your life is in there, and it is as essential as food and water. The Book of Romans also tells us we should follow Paul's example in prayer. Thank God for your life and the good things he brings to it. Release control and let God do the steering.

Tyler (17)

Q. Have you ever asked Kelly's question? Does Tyler's answer help you? What answer would you give?

A. Answers will vary. Invite various teens to share their responses.

Explain: **We know the Bible has answers. Yet, so often we want to seek things out for ourselves. But the reality of "how?" is often overlooked, especially for teens like you who are yet to have careers or even college majors. Tyler does have a good point, though, when he mentions reading the Bible and asks, "Have you actually done it?" Oftentimes, we pick and choose what we want to hear out of the Bible instead of reading it in context and seeing how God works his will through people's lives in real time. Nobody made it into the Bible by accident. We can learn a great deal by examining each life written about in God's Word.**

We can learn a great deal by examining each life written about in God's Word.

Have a volunteer look up Proverbs 3:5 and read it aloud.

"Trust in the Lord with ALL your heart and lean not on your own understanding; in all your ways acknowledge him, and he will make your paths straight."

Ask teens to explain what this verse means to them personally, especially related to finding God's will. You may want to share personal experiences to show your group how God has worked in your life and shown you his will for your life. Your personal testimony may deeply impact your teens, especially if you can relate instances from your teenage years and show how they've molded you into who you are today. (Caveat: Your positive, real-life choices help teens. But be selective when sharing all of your past experiences with your group. As an adult, you've had the benefit of hindsight and reflection. Your teens have not. You do not wish to inadvertently give them permission to go out and try some of your poor life choices.)

END

Have teens turn to "Godfidential" Am I alive? on page 6 of the Guys' section of *Acquire the Fire*. Have a few teens take turns reading the copy, then discuss:

Q. **Why do you think it is important to ask the question, "Am I living?" when it is such an obvious one?**

A. Of course you are alive and taking breaths...but the true question here is, who or what are you living for? Is it for you? A driver's license? Your friends? Your parents' approval? To find a significant other? To serve Jesus? By truly examining our motives we can find our purpose for living and see if God's will is being acted out in our lives.

Q. What are you passionate about? How could those things point you toward God's will for your life?

A. Have teens go around and share some of their passions.

Be aware that some in your group might not be able to come up with something they are passionate about. That's okay. Explain that no matter what our age, we continue to grow and change. Living passionately for Christ is a process of discovery. Go on to explain that God doesn't always speak to us in words, telling us what he wants us to do in life. In fact, that rarely happens. We are, however, given opportunities, relationships, prayer-filled insight, ability, and talents that nudge us in a life-direction.

Living passionately for Christ is a process of discovery.

Have a teen look up and read Psalm 57:2-3 aloud.

"I cry out to God Most High, to God, who fulfills his purpose for me. He sends from heaven and saves me, rebuking those who hotly pursue me; God sends his love and his faithfulness." Explain: **The world is hostile to God and his ways. In today's culture, our life purpose has become diluted by our obsession with money, sex, and our addiction to a "hot" appearance and peer approval. Know this: God is the purpose for our lives. He alone fills the empty place, the longing we feel to be complete, whole, cherished, and purpose-filled. No matter how hard we try, this space cannot be filled by friends, a boyfriend/girlfriend, clothes, gadgets, cars, or even a top-notch SAT score.**

Why? The ache is God-created and God-filled. He alone can answer your most burning question, "Why am I here?" *You're here because God put you here.* Your future rests in his hands. Mention that Jesus knew God's purpose for him all along. Maybe that is one reason that 33 years (Jesus' life on earth) was all he needed to do what he needed to do. God will make it clear to each and every one in your group what he desires for him or her to do. They, on the other hand, need to be open and willing to do it.

Close your time together with a prayer like this one:

God, we are searchers, wanderers—always looking for the thing that will define us and set us apart. Help us discover that your heart is the basis for our life journey. Soften the feelings of inadequacy and doubt that distract us from our life-purpose. We know Jesus prayed, "your will be done." We pray that prayer as well. We patiently wait for "your will be done" in our lives. In Jesus' name, amen.

YOU BECOME WHAT YOU VALUE

Bible Truth:
Value God's choices.

Bible Verse:
"I have chosen the way of truth; I have set my heart on your laws" (Psalm 119:30).

Stuff: Bibles, scenario cards (written ahead of time on index cards)

LESSON THREE

BEGINNING

As you begin your devotional time together, pray that your teens will begin to trust and act on their godly values, using them to shape their lives. Invite members of your group to share prayer requests. Have one or two volunteers pray aloud for these requests.

(Prior to group time, write the following scenarios on two index cards.)

1) *Your best friend leaves a close circle of friends because of a bitter disagreement with one of them. With him/her gone you feel you can no longer be part of the group. Yet you hate to risk losing the benefits of those other friendships. What do you do? Are you truthful or do you fake it? Explain your answer.*

2) *Your parents have made it absolutely clear that you can't have friends over when they aren't home. When last summer's blockbuster hit comes out on DVD everyone is quick to designate your house as the place to watch it. Your parents are at your little brother's open house and will be gone most of the afternoon. What do you choose to do? Have everyone over, knowing they'll be gone long before your parents get home? Can you say no? Explain your answer.*

Divide the group in two. Give scenario one to the first group and scenario two to the second group. Have teens discuss the issues and come up with a few practical applications to these dilemmas. Get back together and have both groups designate a speaker to share on their behalf what they'd do if they were in this situation.

After groups have shared, explain: **We make value choices every day whether we call them that or not. Sometimes situations seem to have no consequences at first glance, but reality paints a different picture. Pretending an allegiance with a group may not score a "1" on a "Top Ten" list of wrongs, but it will have a devastating effect on the integrity of your friendships. Sneaking a few friends in to watch a movie isn't the end of the world, but what about the effect it will have on the relationship you have with your parents? It begs the question, "What do you value?" Moral dilemmas are** unavoidable in everyday life. The choices we make—even choosing to do nothing is a choice—determines what we stand for, what we believe in. When based on biblical principles, our values guide us in real-life situations. *Why is this stuff so important?* The world doesn't share your Christian values. That's why the teenage years are so important. You are becoming who you will be for *life*.

MIDDLE

Ask your group to turn to "Need2Know" Obeying—It's Your Call on page 14 of the Girls' section of *Acquire the Fire,* Issue 2. Have a teen read the opening paragraph aloud. Then discuss:

Q. Do you think teens are guilty of rationalizing sin by saying it's no big deal? What kinds of things fit into this category?

A. Your group might mention things like: copying homework answers, telling white lies, sharing term papers, lifting ideas off the Internet and claiming them, dressing suggestively, physical relationships between guys and girls, breaking their parents' rules at home, etc.

Have a few more teens read the paragraphs on page 14 related to the story of Ananias and Sapphira. If time allows, read the Bible story found in Acts 5:1-10. Have your group contemplate the questions below:

Q. Do you think Ananias and Sapphira thought they were going against God by their actions?

A. Teens may have different opinions. Some may say Ananias and Sapphira *must* have known they were sinning. Others might say it didn't seem like *that* big of a deal…maybe they thought they could blow it off.

Q. Do you think God acted fairly in his treatment of Ananias and Sapphira?

A. Most everyone will probably say that the punishment seems too harsh for the crime. Remind teens that God is just and *all* sin separates us from him. Although we often justify things in our minds as being "really bad," or "mostly OK," God doesn't think as we do. Thankfully, Jesus Christ died in our place and rose again. That is why we don't have to cower before God after every sin we commit. We can confess our sins and find forgiveness. But the truth remains God is holy and he can't excuse sin.

Next have your teens look inward and reflect on their view of sin and their own values.

Q. **How difficult is it for you to look honestly at your sins? Why do we justify our sinful behavior? Why should you care?**

A. Teens will have varying answers. You may find that teens are honest with themselves but when confronted by a parent, teacher, or friend, may find themselves getting defensive or trying to cover up wrongs. Many teens refuse to take responsibility for their behavior, preferring to place the blame on parents, teachers, and those around them.

God is holy. He can't excuse sin.

Q. **Does your conscience bother you after you've done something wrong? What about the second time you do it? Does sinful behavior get easier over time? What does *that* say to you?**

A. Most teens will be aware of their conscience. Teens might say they can tell their face is flushed, feel sick to their stomach, feel nervous, can't eat, have trouble sleeping. Others may say they don't really think about it.

Q. **The Holy Spirit is active and alive in all believers. Do you think your feelings might actually be the Holy Spirit working within you? What other ways might he use to remind you of your values?**

A. Teens may not have thought about this before; they might not realize that the Holy Spirit can use their own feelings to convict them of sin. The values they have (based on what they have learned and applied from the Bible) often come to the surface when they, as Christians, are faced with a moral choice or dilemma. The Holy Spirit can use these things to remind them what they should do in various situations.

Say, **In Acts 5:3 Peter said to Ananias, "How is it that Satan has so filled your heart that you have lied to the Holy Spirit and have kept for yourself some of the money you received for the land?" In Ananias' case, he possessed the gift of the Holy Spirit, but he thought he could deceive him along with everyone else. What we need to remember is that the Holy Spirit knows when we go our own way. We may hide our actions from ourselves, pretending that everything is okay, but the Holy Spirit knows the truth. Still, he yearns to draw us back to a close relationship with God. He stands ready to remind us of our values and prod us when we stray. It's an absolutely good thing to be in touch with the Holy Spirit. He has our very best interest at heart.**

Have your group turn to "Up-In-Out" Knowing Right and Wrong on page 17 in the Girls' section of *Acquire the Fire*. Ask a volunteer to read the first paragraph, Hebrews 8:10–11, aloud.

Say, **Philippians 2:10–11 says, "that at the name of Jesus *every* knee should bow, in heaven and on earth and under the earth, and *every* tongue confess that Jesus Christ is Lord, to the glory of God the Father. God has given us his values, spelled out clearly in the Bible. We can make *his* values *our* values, and in doing so, resist our nature of sin and align with him. Knowing God intimately and taking on his character is the way he intends for us to live purpose-filled lives.**

Have two volunteers read the next two paragraphs of "Up-In-Out" on page 16. Discuss:

Q. What do you think it means to put God's laws in our minds and write them on our hearts?

A. It means we need to apply God's Word in everyday situations. It requires memorization as well as application.

Q. How do you feel when you meet someone who doesn't have the same values as you do? Can you be a positive influence on people who don't share your values?

A. Answers will vary, but some teens might say they are uncomfortable. Others, on the other hand, might feel that it isn't really their business to tell others how to live. Teens might have learned first-hand how their lifestyles can impact those around them. Invite teens to share real-life examples.

Say, **Your godly values make you men or women of integrity. Imagine for a moment "putting on" God's values, as you would a new sweatshirt or jacket. Suddenly your look has changed. When that happens, others can't help but notice. To stand up for right and to refuse to participate in wrong is what God demands from those who follow him. Yes, there's a good chance that your popularity will take a hit. But with God, there is no other way.**

Close your time together with a prayer such as this one:

Dear Jesus, living a life of moral values conflicts with the ways of our sinful world—and we live in the world. Society mocks what you teach and dishonors what you honor. Strengthen us so that we make a difference by holding true to your laws and truths. We trust the Holy Spirit to counsel, guide, and strengthen us. In Jesus' name, amen.

INTEGRITY MATTERS

LESSON FOUR

Bible Truth:
Live a life of truth.

Bible Verse:
"If you love me, you will obey what I command" (John 14:15).

Stuff: Bibles, white board, marker

BEGINNING

As you begin your devotional time together, pray for courage to be a leader. Pray also for your teens to follow Jesus even when it seems the most unnatural thing for them to do. Invite members of your group to share prayer requests if they are comfortable doing so. Have one or two of the students pray aloud for the requests.

Q. Is there a difference between how your Christian friends act and how your non-Christian friends act?

A. Answers will vary.

Q. Do you find it embarrassing when Christians know little about the Bible? Do you feel uneasy when you hear a retelling of a Bible story with little understanding of the story's truth? Why or why not?

A. Answers will be different for different teens. Some may say that they can't believe how ignorant fellow Christians are when it comes to what the Bible says.

Optional Activity

Explain that you will list on the board teen behavior that is contrary to God's law. Your group is to come up with a percentage of teens (that they know personally) that actually engage in that behavior. Have teens think of friends, teens at school, in their neighborhood, clubs, members of their sports teams, etc. Give an example to get things rolling. If the word is "cheating," and they think that half of their peers do it, then they should shout out 50%. Call out the topics below:

Smoking	Stealing
Drugs	Swearing (using
Sex	God's name
Lying to parents	in vain)
Gossip	Cheating

Say, **A recent Gallup Poll stated that fewer than half of the 1,002 youths polled knew that Jesus turned water into wine at the Cana wedding, and nearly two-thirds couldn't identify a quote from Jesus' Sermon on the Mount. About one in ten thought Moses was one of Jesus' 12 apostles.** (News Services, *Gazette Telegraph*, May 1, 2005).

Christian or not, many teens don't know the Bible. How can we live out the Bible if we don't know what's in it?

Summarize this activity by saying; **Fact: Teens make choices that are contrary to God's values. With this reality in mind, let's take a look at the issues in this lesson.**

MIDDLE

Have everyone turn to "Man-datory" on page 19 in the Guys' section of *Acquire the Fire.* Ask two volunteers to read the first section (prior to the bulleted copy) aloud.

Say, **Old Testament David was really something else. He killed a lion and a bear when he was just a boy. He was a giant-slayer. He was also best friends with a guy whose father wanted to kill him. Incredible, isn't it? And there's more. At times in his life, David's conduct was severely lacking in the moral department. One day, he spied on a beautiful married woman as she took a bath. He shouldn't have been looking, but that was the least of it. He later had sex with her, and she became pregnant. Worse still, David had her husband killed, then covered it up so it looked like an accident. Then he married the beautiful woman. Doesn't sound much like a Bible hero, does it? Yet after all that, God still described David as "a man after his own heart" (Acts 13:22). Amazing but true.**

Q. What makes even God's chosen fall to lust and temptation?

A. David was a sinful being. David knew that what he was doing was wrong, but he went ahead with it anyway. Maybe he felt that God wasn't looking. Or that he would make an exception in his case. What he wanted (Bathsheba) was more important than obeying God. He wanted what he wanted.

Have three more volunteers read the bulleted copy. Then discuss:

25

Q. Although God grieved David's sinful choices, how does it make you feel to know that God had a plan and purpose for David's life?

A. Teens might say it helps them understand God's forgiveness; it gives them hope that they can't screw up so badly that God won't want them any longer; it helps them see God's love. God knows better than we do who's right for the job.

Q. Do you think the consequence that David paid (the death of Bathsheba's baby) was too harsh, or did it fit the crime?

A. Some teens that know the story may say David showed remorse by praying and fasting so it seems God should have forgiven him and let the baby live. Others might say God wanted David to learn from his mistake and allowed the death so David would never do something like that again. Remind teens that God is just and that he also can see the big picture, which is something we can't do.

God knows better than we do who's right for the job.

Say, **David and Bathsheba's marriage brought about the line into which Jesus would one day be born. Throughout the Bible, God used flawed and imperfect beings to put into action his will on earth. And he does the same today. Does that mean we happily go about doing wrong because God will use us anyway? No. But when we do wrong, we don't call it quits either. Instead, we pick up the pieces and return to the values defined and made known by God's character according to his Word.**

Q. Do you have any true-life examples of how God used consequences in your life to turn you back to him?

A. Invite volunteers to share. Answers will vary. If teens don't share, try to give an example from your life to help them see how God works all things for good.

Say, **We all mess up. Perhaps not as badly as David did, but we sin nonetheless. David's story has a God-ending because God deemed David the perfect choice to fulfill a higher plan. The same is true for you.**

END

Have teens turn to page 23 in the Guys' section of *Acquire the Fire.* Have teens read the page to themselves.

Q. Does this page strike a chord with you? Do you find that your Christian friends act on what the Bible says or do they do what feels right to them?

A. Answers will be different depending on your teens' friends and peer groups.

Again remind teens that it is common for Christians and non-Christians to score similarly on quizzes or surveys such as this one. Even divorce rates for Christians and non-Christians have proven to be similar. Invite teens to think about what this really means for them as people of faith in a society where individual choice often challenges God's holy law.

Q. How might understanding the responsibilities of being a Christian—and the conduct and life choices that go with it—impact your peers as they see Christ demonstrated through you?

A. Teens might mention that they can really impact people by acting on (not just speaking about) their moral values. Although some people might make fun of them, people who stand by their convictions impress others.

Although peers might make fun of them, teens who stand by their convictions impress others.

Close your time together
with a prayer such as this one:

Lord, this is tough stuff. It's a battle to take the high road when no one else does. We don't want to be labeled lame or a "Jesus freak" or be left out of parties because others put down what we believe. Still, we can't serve two masters. Only through you and your grace and goodness can we live lives of purpose and integrity. Help us to be people of value and honor; we know it is what you want for those who trust in you. In Jesus' name, amen.

Have your students pair up and offer to pray for one another this week. Encourage teens to follow through in praying for each other. Explain that it can really make a difference to know that someone is praying for you and that prayer has power!

MIND-ALTERING RENEWAL

Bible Truth:
Renew your mind with God's eternal truth.

Bible Verse:
"Do not conform any longer to the pattern of this world, but be transformed by the renewing of your mind" (Romans 12:2).

Stuff: Bibles, paper, pens

LESSON FIVE

BEGINNING

As you start your devotional time together, ask God to help your teens reflect and evaluate their self-worth from Christ's point of view. In other words, what might he say to encourage them if he met them on the street? Have your group share prayer requests. Have one or two volunteers pray aloud.

Q. How many people know the real you?

A. Teens might mention their best friends, parents, a grandparent, boyfriend, or girlfriend, siblings, a youth pastor or mentor.

Q. As a youth leader, I've known many teens. I've known teens that can appear hard on the outside but be soft and cuddly on the inside. I've known teens that can be predictable in class yet full of surprises on a youth rally weekend. Above all, I've learned that to really get to know a teen's heart, I need to spend time with him or her. Why is it so hard for each of you to be yourself in today's world?

A. Some answers might be: People are hard to get to know, It takes time to feel comfortable, it's scary to show my real self and/or weaknesses to just anyone, I'm afraid of what others think of me, etc.

Optional Activity

Using pen and paper, have teens describe themselves using words or pictures. Instruct them that on one side of the paper they are to explore their "internal self"—who they feel they are inside. On the flip side, their "external self"—how they show themselves to the world. Explain that although people look at the physical when they see someone, God looks inward first. It's important to remember that although society is preoccupied with look-perfection and status, God doesn't give those things any thought. He is concerned with our hearts and the renewing of our minds.

Q. To what extent does our self-worth, our perception of ourselves, influence what we allow others to know about us?

A. Teens might mention that people with healthy self-esteem or a comfortable self-image are more likely to allow their true self to show. On the other hand, without confidence, we're likely to hide our inner self from others.

MIDDLE

Ask everyone to turn to "Faith on Fire" Renew on page 27 of the Girls' section of *Acquire the Fire*. Have four teens volunteer to read the four paragraphs aloud.

Return to paragraph one and take another look at Ephesians 1:11. Ask:

Q. Do you think friends define their self-worth by who they are in Christ? If not, in whom?

A. Answers might include: the media, what their family thinks about them, what friends at school say, how their boyfriend/girlfriend makes them feel, their own view of themselves (positive or negative), etc.

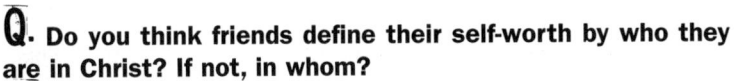

Q. How about you? In whom or what do you find your self-worth?

A. Answers might include: God, the Bible, parents, siblings, friends, school clubs or activities, themselves. There are no wrong answers here, but try to help teens see that the Bible says that it is in Christ that they find out who they really are. Remind them that other people or things can help them build themselves up in positive ways, but ultimately they need to have a relationship with Christ in order to find fulfillment.

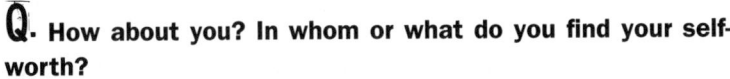

Have the group take another look at the second paragraph. Then ask:

Q. Christ+you = glory. What do you think that equation might look like for you? Define your answer based on Ephesians 1:1.

A. Some possible answers might be: Christ living in me makes my life worth something, Jesus shining out of me makes people take notice, I'm different from non-Christians because of Christ in me, what I do doesn't matter as much as who I am in Christ.

Lastly, look at the fourth paragraph. Ask teens:

Q. **What is one tangible way you can start to renew your mind?**

A. Answers might include: reading the Bible, praying, changing behavior and habits that keep us from growing, making the decision to have a new outlook on life that includes Christ, focusing on eternity, handing over fears to God, memorizing his holy and perfect Word.

Mention to teens that God's idea of renewing their minds is much different from the world or media's view. Say, **Our culture would like us to look to the natural world and use "experience" as the way to life-changing renewal. Experiences such as pre-marital sex, wealth, popularity, star-status and the need for an ultra-cool ride are all things that culture tells us will "get us there." The advice here: be careful about what things you use to renew your mind. God's Word renews and refreshes unconditionally and without disappointment. When taken to heart, it is a gift beyond measure.**

God's Word renews and refreshes without disappointment.

END

Have everyone turn to "Truth & Dare" on page 32 in the Girls' section of *Acquire the Fire.* Have someone read the story depicted in the truth section. (You may also choose to have teens read the article, "Cutting Into the Heart of God," starting on p. 25.)

Ask teens what they know about the practice of cutting (using razors or pins to mark and scar the body).

Q. **Why do teens choose to cut their skin?**

A. It makes them feel better for a short time; it takes their mind off of their inner pain; it's a distraction; they do it to get attention; it's a pain they can control, etc.

Q. In the story, what do you think about how Jen handled the situation?

A. Some teens might say she did a good job of reaching out to her friend. Others might not have thought that her actions were drastic enough considering her friend was hurting herself.

Q. Which of the verses in the prayer journal would impact you the most if you were going through a difficult time?

A. Answers will vary.

Have one of the group members read the "Dare" section aloud.

Q. Do you have friends who suffer from depression? How would you define depression? Explain your answer.

A. Teens will differ on their answers to this question. Remind teens of what they can do if they or a friend is suffering from what they believe is depression. First, acknowledge the courage it took for a friend to bring up the subject. Secondly, assure that person that he or she is not alone and that help is available. Chronic depression is a medical condition that requires medical intervention. Advise your teens not to go it alone but to seek help from trusted adults.

Chronic depression is a medical condition that requires medical intervention.

Q. What do you think should be done to help the 15% - 30% of depressed teens who go on to actually make a suicide attempt?

A. Most teens will say that they need to be reached—somehow; parents should be told so they can help; most teens will agree that talking to a counselor is a very good move since most depression-related incidents have deep roots and are difficult for any teen to solve in just a conversation or two.

Mention that if 20% of teens polled thought about depression it is likely that some in this group have too. Mention that you and other people in your group and church are available if anyone needs to talk. Even if teens aren't feeling severely depressed, they could be suffering from minor depression. Not being able to sleep or sleeping all the time; not wanting to eat or eating all the time; these are just a few symptoms of depression.

Say, **If anyone in this group has any questions about how they've been feeling or if you are experiencing something painful or hurtful, let me or another staff member know. Even if I can't help you directly with your problem, I can put you in touch with someone who can. God gave us feelings; feeling depressed is nothing to be ashamed of, but it is important to take measures and problem-solve issues before things go from bad to worse.**

End your time by having group members close their eyes while you read "The Super Natural Power of Prayer" *Love No Matter What* on p. 31, Girls' section of *Acquire the Fire* aloud. Encourage teens to meditate on these words taken from Psalm 138 and use them to renew their minds as they consider how God sees them in his eternal picture.

Close with a short prayer of your own:

With your holy words we renew our minds and hearts and commit to help others do the same. In Jesus' name, amen.

Bible Truth:
Find your worth in God according to his Word.

Bible Verse:
"'The rain came down, the streams rose, and the winds blew and beat against that house; yet it did not fall, because it had its foundation on the rock'" (Matthew 7:25).

Stuff: Bibles, paper, colorful markers or pencils, stapler

LESSON SIX

BEGINNING

As you start your devotional time together, ask God to give you wisdom as you deal with the very tough topic of self-worth. Invite members of your group to share prayer requests. Have one or two volunteers pray for these requests.

Say, **Although we *know* each other, we don't *really* know everything that is going on inside, do we?** Pause. **Some of you may be feeling awesome today because you got a hefty allowance from your parents, your grades are all A's and B's, and your team just made the state playoffs. Others of you...not quite so good, maybe you got into a fight with your mom or you've dented the fender on dad's car—again. On the outside we all look about the same, but inside, that's another story. Too often we gauge our self-worth on how we handle life-stuff. Did we handle it well? Did we come up with the right solution? How did we look doing it? What must others think of us? Self-worth is an emotional topic. But...it really doesn't have to be. Not when we find our worth in God according to his Word.**

Optional Activity

Pass out paper and have your teens design a feeling-and-prayer journal. Fold an 8 1/2 X 11 sheet widthwise and insert extra sheets to make a simple booklet. Or provide materials to have teens make elaborate journals. Teens can design their journals choosing colors to match their feelings and finish each page with encouraging Scripture verses found inside the Bible or the devotional magazine.

Have a little quiet time and have your teens pinpoint how they are feeling right now. If you wish, have teens go around and ask each other questions that can only be answered with a "yes" or "no" in an effort to gauge the emotion that an individual is feeling. For example, "Do you feel like smiling?" "Are you mad at someone right now?" "Did something bad happen on your way here?" and so on. If a teen's emotion is correctly guessed, have him or her confirm it.

Q. Do you think you'll still feel this way in an hour? Later today?

A. Don't be surprised if teens say they think they'll feel a certain way for hours, even days on end. Teens have powerful feelings. Don't question what they say, rather encourage them by noting that their feelings will pass, whether happy or sad. That is how God made us—emotional beings. But emotion is only a part of who we are. Our emotions work alongside our intellect, abilities and spiritual beliefs to help balance our world. Remind teens that their self-worth should stem from issues deeper than their immediate feelings about themselves.

Summarize this section by saying: **God understands the power of feelings. Yet, he doesn't ever wish us to turn our feelings into a weapon to harm ourselves. Self-doubt and overly critical self-judgment weaken our self-worth. So do the destructive actions of cutting, bulimia, pre-marital sex, binge drinking, illegal drugs, and the overwhelming desire for "look-perfection." Let's remember that our purpose and fulfillment comes from a loving Creator who understands our heart-of-hearts and defines who we are to become.**

MIDDLE

Ask everyone to turn to "Need2Know" How Can I? on page 24 of the Guys' section of *Acquire the Fire*. Have a few volunteers read it aloud.

Q. How do you think Gideon felt when God called him to lead? Does God call leaders today?

A. Gideon wasn't a man who possessed much self-worth. He may have felt terrified at the prospect of being forced to lead. Explain that he didn't let his emotions control him; instead, he obeyed God even when it meant doing something contrary to what his emotions were telling him. God is at work today as he was in the Old Testament.

Q. God's kingdom is here on earth. He's with us always. How can that help when our emotions are painfully scattered and broken?

A. Believing God is with us means having faith that he accompanies us through difficult situations, regardless of how we feel. Knowing God is near can help us keep him as our foundation and help us not be influenced by temporarily intense feelings and emotions. It can help us be grounded in our faith and base our self-worth on how God sees us instead of how we see ourselves.

END

Have everyone turn to "Godfidential" Crying Is For Saviors" on page 25 in the Guys' section of *Acquire the Fire,* Issue 2. Ask a volunteer to read John 11:35 at the top of the section.

Direct these questions to girls and guys alike.

Q. Men often hide their tears. Why?

A. Society, dads, friends, and other guys typically say "don't cry" or that crying is for sissies, losers, or whiners. They tell guys to "suck it up." When little boys get hurt, their parents sometimes ignore the hurt and try to hurry up the happiness. This can be true for girls as well, but is often pushed harder on guys.

Q. Share a time you cried in public. What happened? How did you feel about showing your emotions?

A. Answers will vary. Shameful may be a repeated response. Explain that opening up is hard and we need to respect those who do by our actions, words, and confidentiality. Allow teens (both girls and guys) to volunteer to share about a time when they found themselves crying in front of other people.

Ask a teen to read the second paragraph detailing how Jesus wept.

Q. Jesus wept at his friend Lazarus' death. What does that say to us about the Son of God?

A. Jesus (both God and man) was overcome with sadness, not only for the death of his friend, but very possibly about death in general and the devastation it causes for all who experience the loss of a loved one.

Q. Jesus experienced sadness that cut his heart deeply. How does this empower you to go to Jesus baring your hurts and pain?

A. Jesus empathized with those who were mourning. He was overcome with emotion at the death of a close friend. There are times when crying and hurting is simply part of how life is here on earth. Jesus understood the pain of separation from the core of his being. When it came time for him to die on the the cross, he suffered excruciating pain all while separated from his Father in heaven. Jesus willingly became a sacrificial lamb to save us from our sins. In other words, he became the greatest scapegoat that ever lived. Who better to understand the intense burden that loss and separation place on us?

Say, **One thing we do know, Jesus wasn't thinking about how his tears would look to the crowd.** Ask a volunteer to read the last paragraph aloud.

Q. Jesus wasn't ashamed to show how he felt about the loss of a good friend. How do his tears empower you?

A. Teens may mention Jesus also had concern for Lazarus' friends and may have been expressing to them how much he cared for their feelings as well. Tears often indicate the depth of a special bond or connection.

> Jesus willingly became a sacrificial lamb to save us from our sins. In other words, he became the greatest scapegoat that ever lived.

Q. Might crying be a way for God to heal and cleanse us from the inside out? Explain your answer.

A. Crying isn't something we take lightly—it's exhausting physically and emotionally. For some of us, especially guys, it may make us feel down on ourselves even though we know it is good to do from time to time. We need to ask ourselves why we let it make us feel this way. After all, God designed crying. Jesus cried to release his emotions and wasn't ashamed about it. If Jesus had no problem doing it, we shouldn't either.

Say, **Emotions are a part of life. Jesus experienced them. He understands what you're going through.** Ask a volunteer to share about the incident where Jesus became angry with the moneychangers in the temple. (The complete story can be found in John 2:13-17.)

Q. Jesus became angry—without sinning. In other words, his actions were pleasing to God. Have you ever witnessed righteous anger?

A. Listen to all responses. Teens may bring up the picketing of abortion clinics or the shouts of support to save the lives of death-row inmates. Jesus was upset with what the moneychangers were doing because it went against everything God envisioned for his temple. Jesus also was fulfilling Scripture and showing the disciples that he was the Messiah. (See John 2:17 where the disciples quote from Psalm 69:9.) Jesus also prayed to his Father all the time, which kept him in touch with the will of God.

Q. Holy Scripture tells us that Jesus was "a man of sorrows." He experienced rejection, sadness and tears, and, before his crucifixion, intense anxiety. Yet, his gospel is one of forgiveness, love, joy, compassion and peace. "Whoever lives in love lives in God, and God in him" (1 John 4:16). How can this verse help energize you? Explain.

A. Answers will vary.

Say, **God's truth stands the test of time. He says you're worthy and you are. Generations come and go, cultures rise and fall; yet the Rock of Ages remains. "The rain came down, the streams rose, and the winds blew and beat against that house; yet it did not fall, because it had its foundation on the rock'"** (Matthew 7:25).

Close your time together with a prayer like this one:

Jesus, you made us—up-and-down feelings and all. Help us to honor you with our emotions and yet not allow them to strip away the self-esteem we need to live courageous lives. By putting you at the center of our lives—as our living rock—we have hope and direction. In your name we pray, amen.

A SATISFYING LIFE

Bible Truth:
Be content in all situations.

Bible Verse:
"I know what it is to be in need, and I know what it is to have plenty. I have learned the secret of being content in any and every situation" (Philippians 4:12).

Stuff: Bibles, paper, pens, twenty-dollar bill

LESSON SEVEN

41

BEGINNING

As you begin your devotional time together, pray and ask God to help you reflect on the issue of contentment and how you relate to it. Do you wish for a bigger home, car, paycheck, or "pats on the back" in order to fill the desires of your heart? Where does God fit in? Invite members of your group to share prayer requests if they are comfortable doing so. Have one or two volunteers pray aloud.

Hold up the twenty-dollar bill. Have each member of your group brainstorm what they would buy if they had twenty dollars. (You may want to hand out paper and pens so teens can "do the math.") *Mention that they may not consider twenty dollars much money, but encourage creativity down to the last penny.* Allow a few minutes for your teens to do this. Go around the group and allow as many teens as possible to share their answers.

Say, **A twenty-dollar bill doesn't seem like much, but if one is being handed out you want it, right? On television not long ago, a news team placed a "money tree" on the corner of a busy downtown intersection. The object was to see how people would react to free money. At first, people were hesitant and walked by the tree, not touching it. But as soon as one person pulled off a one-dollar bill, more and more people ran to the tree to grab at the money. The idea of money is always attractive. After all, what's a birthday card without a check inside? Or at least a gift card so you can buy something you want.**

Q. **Everyone wants money. Why do you think money holds such tremendous appeal no matter where you live in the world?**
A. It allows one to survive; it allows flexibility in spending; it seems better than stuff; it feels more real than a credit card.

Q. **Do you have your own credit card or know teens who do? Do you think living on credit is an acceptable life choice for teens, or is it a dangerous way to start out?**
A. Most teens won't have their own credit cards, but a few of their friends might. Some teens may have access to their parents' cards with a designated spending limit. Teens might not really get the idea of a credit card. They may see no harm in using one, even if it isn't paid off each month.

This may be a great time to help your teens realize that living beyond one's means is never a good idea, even if it is money that will be paid back eventually. Although a credit card is necessary for many households (to get a good credit rating, to rent cars or hotels for trips, to prove to a mortgage company that you can be trusted to make payments on time, etc.), it isn't something that should be taken lightly. Our society is in debt because we make it a habit to live on credit. Help teens see that a pay-later lifestyle may indeed hurt them down the line and could cause problems for them in future relationships with a spouse, employer, family member, or credit agency. Most of all it breeds discontentment with what a person does have, causing a deep-rooted desire to buy more and more.

Optional Activity

Say: **Remember as a child when a few quarters was a lot of money? A dollar was huge, and a five dollar bill—a gold mine! Now it's too easy to demand a $20 from Mom or Dad at every turn, isn't it?** Go back around the group and have teens explain how they get their money (parents, allowance, work, savings, grandparents, etc.). Explain: **Although money and the things we buy with money aren't necessarily bad...they won't keep us "forever" happy. Self-worth should never be tied up in dollar bills. If it is, true contentment will be impossible to maintain.**

Say, **Today we'll look at materialism and the pull it has on us. Think about it: We just can't say no, can we? On our quest for more and more, bigger and better—a life of less struggle and more perks—we miss out on what we are all really searching for: contentment. Our Bible truth for today is a simple one. A content life happens only when we remain in a loving relationship with Jesus Christ.**

MIDDLE

Have everyone turn to "Need 2 Know" Other Envy on page 34 of the Guys' section of *Acquire the Fire,* Issue 2. Have one teen read the entire segment aloud.

Q. **What things do your friends have that you wish for?**

A. Everyone's answer will be different but the underlying theme will be similar. Other people just seem to have better stuff. The grass is always greener on the other side.

Q. **What is the secret of being content, as Paul mentions in Philippians 4:12?**

A. Focusing on God. Praising God for what we have, not wishing for what we don't. Realizing that money is necessary but not the way to happiness or fulfillment.

Have teens turn to Luke 12:16-21 and read the verses aloud.

Q. **What did you get out of this story?**

A. You need to be happy with what you have. It is better to share your wealth with others instead of keeping it all for yourself. Your soul is much more valuable than your stuff.

Encourage teens to think about the things they want—then give those desires over to God. If they do so, it doesn't mean they'll never get those things. It just means that they won't be so preoccupied with them.

END

Have teens turn to "GODfidential" 2 Much Stuff on page 35 of the *Acquire the Fire* Guys' section. Have a teen read Mark 5:26 aloud.

Q. Why do you think this woman spent all she had to get better? Wouldn't you?

A. Being healthy is more important than having things. Why have material things if you can't enjoy them because you are too sick?

Have a different volunteer read the rest of the devo aloud.

Q. What can you learn from this devo?

A. To be happy with what you have; to be thankful for your health; to be more concerned with your relationship with God than your things.

Q. Statistics show that there are about eight million millionaires in the world today. What do you think: If you took a survey, would the rich be happier than the poor? For the purposes of the survey, how would you define the words "rich" and "poor"? More importantly, how would you define the word "happiness"?

> **Rich or poor, contentment is not based on the size of your bank account, car, or the price of your "toys."**

A. Rich or poor, contentment is not based on the size of your bank account, car or the price of your "toys." Ownership of things will not strengthen our values or build godly character, wisdom, and integrity. Rich or poor—this is the real stuff of life.

Say, When I think of "money-as-the-path-to-happiness," I ask myself a few simple questions. You should too. *What price would I pay for happiness? What price would I pay for my soul? Would I accept $1,000,000 dollars to betray the love of a friend? If I inherited great wealth but needed the gift of a kidney from an anonymous donor…where would my happiness lie?* In this day and age, when materialism is the new religion, it's important to be reminded of the truth. Money is essential. And it's fun to spend. But it doesn't buy happiness or contentment: Living within the peace and heart of God does. True contentment is not money-related.

Close your time together with a prayer like this one:

Father, we are blessed for we have more than we need. Our barns are full and over-flowing. With your grace, help us to focus on the internal—faith in you and lives of service to others. Only then can we enjoy the gift of contentment that far outshines the artificial glare of today's materialistic culture. In Jesus' name, amen.

ETERNAL VALUE

Bible Truth:
"You can't take it with you."

Bible Verse:
"But store up for yourselves treasures in heaven, where moth and rust do not destroy, and where thieves do not break in and steal" (Matthew 6:20).

Stuff:
Bibles, white board, markers

LESSON EIGHT

BEGINNING

As you begin your devotional time together pray and ask God to help you take a hard and honest look at material things that you place a great value on and how they conflict with your life of faith. Have members of your group share prayer requests if they have any. Have one or two volunteers pray aloud.

Have your group members think for a minute about what their most treasured possession was when they were younger and what it is now. After teens have had time to reflect, have them share with the group. Write these objects down on one side of the white board with a header that reads, "Kid Stuff." Next have teens share what their treasured possessions are now. Write these down under a header that reads, "Teen Stuff."

Optional Activity

Have your group come up with five things they'd take out of their house if they were told a demolition crew was coming in ten minutes. Go around the group and have different individuals share their responses. Ask teens: **Would your parents take these same five things? How about your brother or sister?** Mention that today's lesson is about things that are important to us. Although material things matter in the short run, what really matters is what we do for Jesus while we live on his earth.

Q. How has your preference for "good stuff" changed over time?

A. Teens might mention that the scruffy stuffed animal or a popular action figure or toy doesn't hold the same appeal to them now. Although it might still have sentimental value, it isn't really important to their lives.

Q. Did the worth or value of the possession change or did *you* change?

A. Teens will say that they changed. As they grew up their priorities shifted and they now desire things that can help them today.

Q. Think about what you treasure now. Picture it in your mind. What value might it still hold in ten years?

A. Some teens might say they'll still treasure this item; others might realize that they'll probably value other things more down the road. One or two might say they don't care about the future. It's the "now" that's important to them.

Say, **Maybe you're really anxious to get a car; *any* set of wheels! Not because you really want a certain make or model but because you'll do *anything* just to have some freedom and not have to rely on your parents to get someplace. Years from now, however, when you're driving your kids around in an S.U.V you'll pretty much take the better ride for granted. Over time, things we wish for lose their appeal. We need to place our emphasis— the way God does—on the eternal.**

MIDDLE

Ask everyone to turn to "girlOUTstanding" No Win Situation on page 40 in the Girls' section of *Acquire the Fire*. Ask someone to read aloud the copy in bold type.

Q. **What is the must-have thing for teen guys today? What about for the girls?**

A. Brand names are very important to teens today. Most teens won't consider buying store brand yogurt, cereal, candy or soda, considering it poor people's food. To own pricey jeans, shoes, pocketbooks sets teens apart and makes them feel special.

Q. **Are there items that you have at home that you really wanted last year that are now out of style? Explain.**

A. Teens might mention last year's name-brand clothes, computer games, and software.

Have a volunteer read the next three paragraphs aloud. Then discuss.

Q. **What few things could you give away and hardly miss?**

A. All teens will say different things. What will likely be the same is that they will each have something that they don't need just sitting around. Encourage teens to get rid of this kind of stuff but make sure they give it to a worthy cause so someone else can benefit from it. Remind teens that people living in western nations have no clue how fortunate we are. Much of the world lives in poverty.

Q. There is one thing you do for others that has value beyond your lifetime. Name it.

A. Bringing others to Christ.

Have a teen read Matthew 6:20 aloud. Then say: **Although we yearn for great stuff and for what others have, we need God and each other more. There are people within our reach who could use a few hours of extra help—younger brothers and sisters, the elderly, a single mom or dad. You can help out by sharing your skills in literacy and after-school programs or your church's Vacation Bible School. And what about your money? Save it and donate a portion to missions or support a child in a poverty-stricken country. In God's eyes, what we do for others is a thousand times more valuable than sitting around admiring our stuff.**

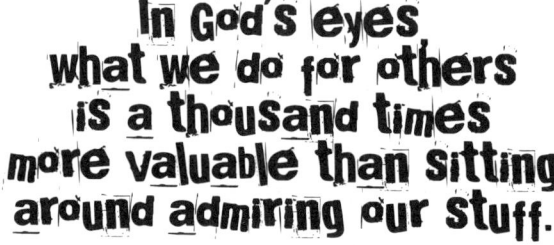
In God's eyes what we do for others is a thousand times more valuable than sitting around admiring our stuff.

END

Have everyone turn to "Truth & Dare" on page 42 in the Girls' section. Have volunteers read the "Truth" and "Dare" sections aloud.

Q. What "griefs" are your peers pierced with as they are consumed with the desire for material things?

A. Teens might mention that teens shoplift to get what they want even if they have the money to buy it. Others might mention general unhappiness, constant comparison of one another, spending money they don't have just to feel good about themselves.

Q. Why would someone give up his or her faith in God in exchange for things?

A. They might not be able to see beyond today. They become sidetracked.

Q. What does "eager for money" mean to you?

A. Money equals power. Money can get you what you want. With enough money you can get ahead in life: afford a good education, a well-paying job, a fancy house, a sporty car, etc.

Teens shoplift to get what they want even if they have the money to buy it.

Have a teen read aloud the statistic at the bottom of the devo page.

According to statistics, the average teen in the United States spends approximately $5,000 per year.

Q. Do you think that amount seems too high or too low? What do you think might happen if you designated one-tenth of that money ($500) to God's work each year?

A. Answers will vary, but encourage teens to think about setting aside a certain amount to see what God can do with it.

End your group time with a prayer like this one:

Heavenly Father, you tell us how we are to live: we are to desire you above all things, die to self-want, strive for godly character, bear fruit and live a life of sacrifice. This is the stuff of life—not the cell phones buzzing in our pockets or the cash, DVDs and jewelry lying on our dressers at home. Create a hunger in our souls to do that which will store up for us treasures in heaven. You are a gracious God and we are truly thankful that we can meditate on your holy Word for direction and strength. In Jesus' name we pray, amen.

THE FAITH FACTOR

Bible Truth:
Trust and have faith in God's calling.

Bible Verses:
"These [trials] have come so that your faith—of greater worth than gold, which perishes even though refined by fire—may be proved genuine and may result in praise, glory and honor when Jesus Christ is revealed" (1 Peter 1:7).

Stuff:
Bibles, poster boards, markers

LESSON NINE

BEGINNING

As you begin your devotional time, ask God to help your teens come to an understanding that motivation can generate from the external pressures of a sinful world or by the internal guiding and whispers of the Holy Spirit. Invite members of your group to share prayer requests. Have one or two group members pray aloud.

Divide your group into smaller groups. Say, **If you could design the life you've always wanted, what would it look like? Take a moment now and as a group use the poster board to chart a perfect life. Include highlights like schooling, salvation, your first car, graduations, a gold-medal win in the upcoming Olympics, travel and mission trips, a career as a world-famous writer or recording artist, marriage, family, retirement, grandchildren, etc. The one downside to your perfect life is that it does have an imperfect end. In other words, be sure to include a date of death.**

After groups have had a chance to map out their person's life, have volunteers share their "perfect lives" with the group.

Q. What thoughts came to mind as you planned the perfect life?

A. I want a perfect life! Fun or awesome. A few teens might say they weren't really affected because it was all made-up. Some might say they felt funny "playing God," and making life choices for someone else. Others might have enjoyed choosing a career, family, and location to live for someone else. Some may have used the experience to reflect on what they want out of life.

Q. Who has played the Parkers Brothers' game called *Life*? What is your favorite part?

A. Answers will vary, but most will probably say it is fun to buy property and to put baby boys (blue pieces) or baby girls (pink pieces) into the car they are driving across the game board.

Say, **Obviously, the major downfall in real life is that we don't know the outcome of the months or the years ahead.** We certainly wish for the best, but it cannot always be plotted or planned that way. Yet we all know the eventual outcome for our lives. As hard as it is for teens to relate to the fact, death is in their future.

Say, **Whether we have an easy life or a life of hard knocks—our days on earth are numbered. Yet, in God we know the game plan: to trust and have faith in his calling. Even if the days, weeks, and months ahead are not what we would have planned for ourselves, or it involves suffering and long stretches of wilderness walking, in God our motivation is clear: live in faith in his big picture world. And *trust* that his superior perspective goes before you. With *faith* you can endure what you must, be courageous when you need to be and hopeful that good things will come from your time here.**

Optional Activity

Have teens turn to page 45 of the Guys' *Acquire the Fire*, Issue 2 and designate someone to read the Q. and A. of the Tribal Wisdom aloud. Have teens reflect on Brian's (age 14) question and David's (age 16) answer. Invite teens to share aloud about how they live their own lives, even though they know things could go wrong or plans could backfire at any time. Ask teens to share how they juggle their own plans and goals. Ask, **how do you know when your life is out of balance? Do you feel it? Do you tend to accept or reject your parents' advice on how to handle it?**

MIDDLE

Have the group turn to "GODfidential" Follow the Leader on page 45 of the Guys' section of *Acquire the Fire*. Ask a volunteer to read the Scripture verse, John 21:20, aloud.

Have any of you ever read this verse before? It isn't a well-known verse, but it is what we are going to focus on today.

Have another volunteer read the rest of the devo aloud. Then discuss:

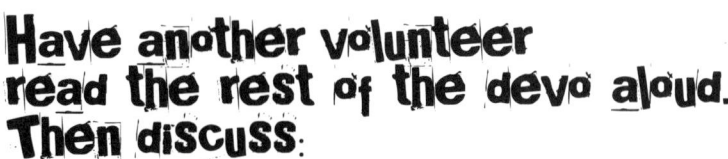

Q. Why do you think John felt it important to mention that he was loved by Jesus?

A. So people would personalize his account of Jesus' life; to give credibility to his account; to express his own love for Jesus; to acknowledge to himself Jesus' love for him.

Q. Why do you think John followed Jesus even though Jesus asked Peter to follow him?

A. John knew that Jesus was worth following. He didn't need to be told.

Q. Why do you think that society gives more respect to leaders than followers?

A. There are more followers than leaders. Leaders demand respect; followers, on the other hand, do just that: follow.

Q. How can following Jesus' example provide excellent motivation for your life?

A. If a person is following Jesus, then everything else in life falls into place. We know why we do the things we do. The Bible also can be a guide and give answers about what a person should do as he or she journeys through life.

Following Jesus means godly companionship and the ultimate reward of eternity in paradise.

Jesus warns his followers that they will have trouble on earth. On the other hand, he promises that those who follow him will have light yokes to carry. (See Matthew 11:28-30.) He also promises never to forsake us. (See Joshua 1:5; Hebrews 13:5). Following Jesus means godly companionship and the ultimate reward of eternity in paradise.

END

Have the group turn to "Faith on Fire" "X" Marks the Spot on page 47 of the Guys' section of *Acquire the Fire.*

Q. Ask teens what they think of the word "extreme." Has it lost its meaning or is it still cutting edge?

A. Answers will vary. Some teens might say they still picture that word with cliff-plunging snowboarders or climbs up Everest. Others, however, may say that they think of extreme pizza toppings or other things.

Q. An extreme life for Christ can mean an uncomfortable life with little financial reward. Why would anyone want to live an extreme life in faith, like Joseph did?

A. It's what we're called to do. It's impossible to have a heart of faith and say "no" to God. By doing the right things, sticking to our convictions, and trusting God's plans, we are promised the good life in him.

Eventually, you'll get to where God wants you to be. Trust in him.

Q. What sorrows do teens face?

A. Answers will vary, but encourage students to answer honestly. They may mention drugs, unplanned pregnancy, abortion, depression, suicide, divorce of parents, loneliness, low self-esteem, etc.

Q. How can teens stay motivated and not lose their spiritual intensity and focus?

A. Everyone will have a different opinion on how they can get motivated. Encourage your group members to act on these suggestions this week and see if they feel any better about the direction they're headed by next week. Eventually, you'll get to where God wants you to be. Pray for direction.

Summarize by saying: **Followers of Jesus discover motivation by living as he did and imitating his lifestyle. What was Jesus' #1 priority? Being focused on his Father. When you feel lost, blah, and unmotivated...the Bible has lots of answers. And, always, give your frustrations to God in prayer and see what he does with them.**

Close your time together with a prayer like this one:

Lord, it's easy to throw up our hands and let discouragement and life events stand in the way of our trust in you. Guide us in your ways and lead us to passages in the Bible that can help us in times when we lack motivation. We want to walk-the-walk and talk-the-talk of our Lord and Savior, Jesus Christ. We ask all of these things in Jesus' name, amen.

EXCELLENT MOTIVATION: GOD'S PLANS

Bible Truth:
God has big plans for your life.

Bible Verse:
"'For I know the plans I have for you, declares the LORD, 'plans to prosper you and not to harm you, plans to give you hope and a future'" (Jeremiah 29:11).

Stuff: Bibles, calendars, white board, pens

LESSON TEN

BEGINNING

As you begin your devotional time, pray that teens will allow themselves the prayer time and patience it takes to discover God's plan for them. Invite members of your group to share prayer requests. Have one or two of the students pray aloud for the requests that have been shared.

Have girls and guys in your group open their devos to the "get it done" Day Planner on p. 4. Have teens plot out a rough schedule of their week: sports practices, work, after-school meetings, student council, music programs or practice, etc.

Regroup and discuss:

Q. **Do you think you are too busy or not busy enough?**

A. Most teens will say they are too busy. They can hardly see straight, never sleep, and are consumed with friends, extra activities, and homework.

Optional Activity

Write on a white board one of the following quotes from teens: *If it feels right and gets me out of bed in the morning, it's purpose enough.* or *I try but I just don't measure up. So why bother?* or *Most stuff is boring. I need thrills to get motivated.* Have teens come up with responses to the quotes above. How would they communicate to their friends a Christian life alive in the Spirit?

Q. **Why do you think teens, in general, like to stay busy?**

A. It is fun; they have no choice; there are lots of things that need to be done now in order to get into a good college or university; work and school take up all their time, etc.

Q. **If you were in control of your schedule (instead of circumstances dictating what you do), would you add things to your schedule or delete entries?**

A. Answers will be different. The majority of teens, however, will likely want to get rid of some of the busyness of their lives and have more time to relax or hang with friends. Hopefully some will mention their desire to spend more time reading the Bible and praying.

Say, **Teens are motivated by lots of things. Fear, competition, independence, popularity, and peer pressure top many a list. Money, appearance, cars, grade reports, and athletic performance come in a close second. Sadly, I've known only a few teens** who have been motivated by a daily spiritual walk with their loving Savior. As you go about your busy week think on this: an over-scheduled calendar will certainly motivate you. But don't allow it to—don't allow busyness to crowd out the connection you have with your spiritual Father. Pray for the truth of his direction. Jeremiah 29:11 says, "'For I know the plans I have for you,' declares the LORD, 'plans to prosper you and not to harm you, plans to give you a hope and a future.'"

MIDDLE

Have the group turn to "Need 2 Know" Check Your Mood on page 44 of the Girls' section of *Acquire the Fire,* Issue 2. Ask a few volunteers to read this section aloud.

Mention that the pressure to get into a good college or have a successful career starts early. (Some of your group may have felt this pressure before they even entered middle school and most are definitely feeling the squeeze now.) It doesn't really matter if your group is all seniors or if they are all freshmen, they probably are still feeling some stress about their futures. Encourage your group members to open up for this discussion and get some of the pressure off their backs.

Q. What are your biggest stresses right now?
A. Answers might include: good grades, finding (or keeping) a boyfriend/girlfriend, getting into college or university or trade school, knowing what they are to do in the future career-wise, fitting in at school, sports teams, work, parents, etc.

Share, **If you are slacking, then it is only reasonable that your teachers or parents get on your case. They want you to succeed, find a good college or trade, and eventually land a great job. You may not see eye-to-eye with them right now on anything. But keep in mind that *they do know* things about life even if you don't think they do.**

Have teens look at the third and fourth paragraphs of the devo again. Then ask:

Q. What kinds of things do you think the Apostle Paul might have worried about?
A. Answers might include: guilt over his former life and the

Christians he had persecuted or killed; his future—since he had lots of enemies; where his next meal was coming from; if he'd have a safe place to stay; if he'd have to go back to prison or even be executed for his faith.

Q. Why is it important to live our lives where we aren't "trying to please men [people] but God, who tests our hearts" (1 Thessalonians 2:4)?

A. We'll never please people no matter how hard we try. If we are focused only on this life and the people in it, we'll fail miserably. If our motive is to follow God and go where he leads—well, then it is much harder to fail because God knows us and has a plan for us.

Q. How does a person's attitude affect his or her life path?

A. A bad attitude is a stumbling block for many teens. It keeps them from growing or seeing things from another's point of view. A person who is always "right," or down or angry or worried is not going to be heading in the direction that God has planned for him or her. Also being moody can cause those around us to be unsure of how to act around us. It could even ruin our testimony because people won't want to become Christians if they can't see joy in the people who claim to be.

If we choose to be true followers of Christ, it is important to be consistent and motivated. We can't be up and down when it comes to our faith. That doesn't do anyone any good.

END

Have everyone turn to "Up/In/Out" on page 46 of the Girls' section of *Acquire the Fire*. Ask a volunteer to read the verse that begins this section. Then have a few more teens read the rest of it aloud.

Q. Can you relate to what Craig (age 16) is saying here?

A. A few teens won't relate, but many will. It is hard to stand out from the crowd and not take part in the partying, drugs, and sex that a number of teens do. This is where faith in God plays in. Because of their faith in him, many teens will refrain from things that they otherwise might be tempted to do.

Q. What keeps *you* from doing these things?

A. Teens might mention their parents, siblings, church, youth group, faith in God. Some might be more honest and admit that they don't do some things for fear of getting caught or because the consequences would be severe. Allow teens to admit that they are tempted at times to do things their peers do. Because we're human, we all fall short of what God would call us to do. God, however, can help us with our human faults and lead us in the way he wants us to go. With God at the helm of our lives, we have reason to be different and to obey his commands, instead of just doing what feels good at the time.

Q. Can you share your testimony of how God has helped you live your life for him?

A. Use this time to invite volunteers to share their testimonies of how God has worked in their lives to help them either turn from worldly things or not get involved in them from the get-go. No one is a better motivator than your teens one-to-another.

Thank teens that shared about their lives and gave their Christian testimonies. Then say: **We're all tempted at times to give up the Christian life. But, we *need* to fight the good fight, *finish* the race, and *get* the promised crown of righteousness. (See 2 Timothy 4:7-8.)**

Close your time together with a prayer like this one:

Father, as we leave today we enter into a time of preparation. We commit to study and grow in the wisdom of your Word. Time spent with you is the only way we'll become motivated to live outside of the world and with you in our hearts. We end our prayer with Jesus' words — "I am the vine; you are the branches. If a man remains in me and I in him, he will bear much fruit; apart from me you can do nothing" (John 15:5). Amen.

The Word at Work Around the World

A vital part of Cook Communications Ministries is our international outreach, Cook Communications Ministries International (CCMI). Your purchase of this book, and of other books and Christian-growth products from Cook, enables CCMI to provide Bibles and Christian literature to people in more than 150 languages in 65 countries.

Cook Communications Ministries is a not-for-profit, self-supporting organization. Revenues from sales of our books, Bible curricula, and other church and home products not only fund our U.S. ministry, but also fund our CCMI ministry around the world. One hundred percent of donations to CCMI go to our international literature programs.

CCMI reaches out internationally in three ways:

· Our premier International Christian Publishing Institute (ICPI) trains leaders from nationally led publishing houses around the world.

· We provide literature for pastors, evangelists, and Christian workers in their national language.

· We reach people at risk—refugees, AIDS victims, street children, and famine victims—with God's Word.

Word Power, God's Power

Faith Kidz, RiverOak, Honor, Life Journey, Victor, NexGen — every time you purchase a book produced by Cook Communications Ministries, you not only meet a vital personal need in your life or in the life of someone you love, but you're also a part of ministering to José in Colombia, Humberto in Chile, Gousa in India, or Lidiane in Brazil. You help make it possible for a pastor in China, a child in Peru, or a mother in West Africa to enjoy a life-changing book. And because you helped, children and adults around the world are learning God's Word and walking in his ways.

Thank you for your partnership in helping to disciple the world. May God bless you with the power of his Word in your life.

For more information about our international ministries, visit www.ccmi.org.